cover to cover

Bible S

7 Sessions for Ho
and Personal

Revelation
4-22

The Lamb wins!
Christ's final victory

Brian Hoare

Published 2006 by CWR, Waverley Abbey House, Waverley Lane, Farnham, Surrey GU9 8EP, UK.

See back of book for list of National Distributors.

Concept development, editing, design and production by CWR

Cover image: Design Pics Inc.

Printed in Spain by Espace

ISBN-10: 1-85345-411-7
ISBN-13: 978-1-85345-411-0

Contents

Introduction

Most of the book of Revelation (despite its title, which means 'unveiling') remains a mystery to many. We are familiar with chapters 1 to 3 (letters to the seven churches) but few of us venture further. It is through that neglected territory (unique in the New Testament) that these studies are designed to guide us.

We may take comfort from the fact that we are not the only people to have found Revelation difficult. For years the Church hesitated to include it in the full canon of Scripture – even Martin Luther would have omitted it from the New Testament! Moreover, once its place was firmly established, over-fanciful and wildly dogmatic interpretations deterred many Christians from persevering with it.

As we remedy that situation in these studies, we consider first some introductory questions about this book. Its opening verses (Rev. 1:1,4,9) state it to be by 'John', traditionally believed to have been John the Apostle – and these studies assume that to be the case. There are both reasons to support that view and difficulties in the way of it, and those interested in such questions should consult the commentaries. No one can be really certain either way. In the case of this particular book, however, who wrote it is of little consequence: its real author is Christ Himself (Rev. 1:1; 22:16). It is a 'revelation of Jesus Christ', and as we read we must constantly look for what it teaches us about Him.

We have already noted that the book of Revelation is unique in the New Testament. We are familiar with the Gospels (recording the ministry and teaching of Jesus); the Acts of the Apostles (describing the infant Church and the spread of the gospel to the Gentiles); and the Epistles (letters by Paul and others to churches and individuals dealing with questions arising in the life of the Early Church). But what about Revelation? It is a mixture of different forms of writing, comprising epistle (Rev. 1:1–4,11), prophecy (Rev. 1:1–3; 22:7,10,18–19) and what is called 'apocalyptic'. Apocalyptic was a form of writing that flourished in the first century AD (though there are Old Testament examples of it in Daniel, Ezekiel and Zechariah) and is characterised by a background of persecution, a recurring use of visions, pictures and numbers and frequent references back to the Old Testament. The danger when reading such literature is to try to interpret every symbol literally or historically. John is a word-artist, and we should see his book not so much as a photograph of future events, but more like an abstract painting whose truth and power lie not in the meaning of every detailed brush stroke but in the overall effect as we stand back and let the whole picture make its impact upon us. Whereas in Old Testament apocalyptic the visions and symbols are almost always interpreted, in Revelation there is a marked absence of explanation. While we shall certainly want to wrestle with some detailed interpretation, our main goal will be to see the overall picture of what this book has to teach us.

The book of Revelation was written at a time when the Church was in conflict with the pagan, secular state and was undergoing terrible persecution. It was meant to offer encouragement to its first readers in that historical setting. To confine its application to that period, however, is to limit the book's usefulness. Conversely, to see it as prophesying wholly future events still centuries ahead (some claim to see Napoleon, Hitler, the Arab–Israeli conflict and even the European Union in its pages) is to render it irrelevant to the first-century Church. Clearly a right understanding of Revelation needs it to apply to every Christian in every culture and in every age. Thus, perhaps one of the most important keys to understanding this book is to recognise that the visions it describes are parallel rather than consecutive pictures of the whole sweep of Christian history from the first to the second coming of Christ.

During a recent visit to Prague I was reminded of a story I heard told by Dr H Eddie Fox, World Director of Evangelism for the World Methodist Council, at a conference in Singapore. Under the Communist regime in former Czechoslovakia the authorities sought to suppress the work of the churches by refusing permission for any external church signs or the ringing of church bells. In 1989, however, the Czech people decided enough was enough and what was termed 'the Velvet Revolution' began. They walked out of their jobs, schools and homes and stood silently with their dream of freedom. They determined that on 27 November at 12 noon they would ring the church bells, and as the bell of the Methodist church in Prague rang out the pastor's wife suggested they should also erect a sign outside the church. It read 'The Lamb wins!'.

That in a nutshell is the message of the book of Revelation. Its grand theme is the ultimate victory of God and His Church over Satan and all his allies. As Revelation 17:14 puts it: 'They will make war against the Lamb, but the Lamb will overcome them because he is Lord of lords and King of kings.' If our studies help us to grasp that truth, however much or little other detail we understand, they will be well worthwhile.

WEEK 1

The Lamb upon the Throne

Opening Icebreaker

Who is the most famous person you have ever met, and what is the most awe-inspiring building you have ever visited? Has anyone met a member of the royal family, or visited Buckingham Palace? What pictures come to mind when you hear the words 'royal throne'?

Bible Reading

Revelation 4:1–5:14

Opening Our Eyes

As John in his vision enters an open door into heaven, he sees something that is central not to these chapters only but to the whole of the book of Revelation: a Lamb seated upon the throne. At first, however, John simply says that 'someone' was sitting on the throne (Rev. 4:2). It is not clear who it is, though since he sits in great splendour and is clearly the object of unceasing worship by those surrounding the throne we may take this to be a picture of God Himself. Those who surround the throne include:

- *The twenty-four elders* (4:4) who may be symbolic of the whole people of God. The 12 patriarchs in the Old Testament and 12 apostles in the New (see also 21:12–14) represent both the old and new dispensations and include both Jews and Gentiles.
- *The four living creatures* (4:6–8 – cf.Ezek. 1:5ff) perhaps represent the whole created world – the lion being the king of wild beasts, the ox supreme among cattle, the eagle the king of birds and man the crown of God's creation. All nature and the whole of humanity praise God!

At the beginning of Revelation 5 we are introduced to the picture of a sealed scroll (again with Old Testament echoes – see Ezek. 2:9–3:3), which we may see as symbolising God's plan of salvation and His purposes for the destiny of the world. The fact that there is writing on both sides suggests that it is full and complete: no detail has been left out. But who is worthy to open it (Rev. 5:2)? God's plan is so far unrevealed and unfulfilled, and John weeps in despair, for no mere mortal can unlock it.

Attention then turns to 'the Lion of the tribe of Judah' (5:5) who is able to open the scroll; but as we look we see not a lion – but a Lamb (5:6,8,12–13). He had once been slain but is now very much alive. He still bears the marks of crucifixion, but tragedy has turned to triumph. Here are meekness and majesty combined. The Lion is never mentioned again (indeed, this precise term is found nowhere else in Scripture), but the Lamb comes to the rescue. He alone is worthy to fulfil God's saving plan. Revelation 5:6 fills out the picture of the Lamb still further: He has seven horns (symbols of strength and honour – Deut. 33:17; Psa. 112:9) and seven eyes (symbols of knowledge – Zech. 4:10). Seven is a symbol of perfection and completeness, and (like other symbolic numbers) occurs many times in Revelation. Here it underlines the fact that the Lamb is all-powerful and all-knowing. No wonder He is 'worthy to take the scroll and to open its seals' (Rev. 5:9)!

So we come to one of the most dramatic moments in the whole book: as the Lamb takes the scroll He is enthroned with God the Father (5:7,13). This is nothing less than the coronation of the Saviour (Heb. 2:9), and the whole universe explodes with praise and worship (Rev. 5:9–14)!

Discussion Starters

1. How many hymns and worship songs can you think of that are based on the songs found in these two chapters?

2. John says he was 'in the Spirit' (4:2; cf.1:10) as he saw this vision. What do you think that means and is it an experience we too might have?

3. John tells us that a rainbow encircled the heavenly throne (4:3). How do other rainbows mentioned in Scripture (Gen. 9:13–15; Ezek. 1:28) help us to understand this picture?

4. Whenever worship is offered in these chapters the worshippers 'fall down' (Rev. 4:10; 5:8,14). What can this teach us about our own attitudes to worship?

5. In the 'Opening Our Eyes' section it was suggested that the 'twenty-four elders' (4:4) represented the whole people of God and the 'four living creatures' (4:6–8) the whole of creation. What alternative interpretations can you suggest?

6. The custom of using incense and candles in some forms of worship perhaps derives from Revelation 5:8. What place or value does such symbolism have in contemporary Christian worship?

---

7. The phrase 'a new song' (5:9) occurs frequently in Scripture (Psa. 40:3; 96:1; 149:1; Isa. 42:10; Rev. 14:3), the word 'new' meaning 'of a new quality' or 'fresh' rather than 'recently written'. What implications does this have for our own use of hymns and songs in worship?

---

8. Revelation 5:9 describes a salvation that is for all regardless of race, language, culture or nationality. Share experiences of being in groups of Christians that spanned those divisions. What bearing does this verse have on racial and class divisions in the Church?

---

9. What does it mean to say that every created being (5:13) praises God? Perhaps Psalm 65:9–13, Psalm 148 and Philippians 2:9–11 might help our answer.

Personal Application

Two pictures in these chapters offer encouragement.
First, *the Lamb upon the throne* – a powerful reminder
to Christians who suffer hardship that God is sovereign.
Whatever difficulties or opposition we face, God is
still on the throne and we are 'more than conquerors
through him who loved us' (Rom. 8:37). Think about
any problems you are currently encountering in your
own Christian life, and try to see them in the light of this
important truth.

Second, *worship is constantly being offered in heaven*. It
is loud and exuberant (Rev. 5:12) and never stops day
or night (4:8). Praise is a good antidote to hardship and
despondency. Remember Paul and Silas singing hymns
at midnight despite being imprisoned in Philippi (Acts
16:25), and learn the secret of praising God in every
circumstance.

Seeing Jesus in the Scriptures

Scripture describes Jesus by many different names, but the
'Lamb of God' is a particularly fruitful theme for study.
Look up such passages as Genesis 22:7–8, Isaiah 53:7,
John 1:29,36, Acts 8:32–35, 1 Corinthians 5:7 and 1 Peter
1:18–19 to see the way this theme is developed. Yet all
these texts refer to a sacrificial lamb, whereas the picture
in Revelation is of a Lamb who, though once slain (Rev.
5:6), is now victorious and seated on the throne as the
object of praise and worship by all the hosts of heaven
(5:6,8,12–13). No wonder the hymn writer wrote of the
'spotless Lamb of God … lifted up to die' who is 'now in
heaven exalted high: Hallelujah! What a Saviour!'

WEEK 2

The Seven Seals

Opening Icebreaker

Has anyone ever had the frustrating experience of not being able to open something that was sealed? Share as many different ways as you can think of to seal a package or parcel. What is the purpose of a seal?

Bible Reading

Revelation 6:1–8:1

Opening Our Eyes

The seven seals were introduced in Revelation 5:1, and
verse 9 showed that only the victorious Lamb could
open them. As He opens the first four seals (6:1–8) we
are introduced to 'the four horsemen of the apocalypse'.
They represent not specific historical people, but events
recurring throughout the whole of human history.

- The *first seal* reveals a rider on a white horse (6:2),
  which some see as Jesus Himself (because of 19:11). It
  is more likely, however, that this is a general picture of
  military conquest.
- The rider of the fiery red horse in the *second seal* (6:3–4)
  destroys peace on the earth. Red signifies blood that is
  always shed in conflict, the 'large sword' symbolising the
  power to kill (Ezek. 21:14; Rom. 13:4).
- The *third seal* reveals a black horse (Rev. 6:5–6)
  symbolising famine in which people are so desperate
  for food that they will pay vastly inflated prices for it.
- The *fourth seal* reveals a pale horse (6:7–8) whose
  meaning is clearly interpreted as death itself.

These four horsemen, then, describe things happening
on earth and represent those four great destructive forces
of warfare, bloodshed, famine and death which Jesus
said would mark the beginning of the end times (Matt.
24:4–14), but which have always characterised human
experience. Now the focus changes from earth to heaven.

- The *fifth seal* reveals the persecuted Church and the
  Christian martyrs (Rev. 6:9). First-century readers would
  recognise the scene – but it also describes those who
  have died for their faith in every age, and the number
  continues to grow (6:11). The cry 'How long?' (6:10)
  and the desire for vengeance are understandable,
  though the cry is not for personal revenge. Vengeance
  belongs to God alone (Rom. 12:19).
- As the *sixth seal* is opened (Rev. 6:12–17) we see

devastating cosmic upheaval reminiscent of passages
such as Joel 2:30–31, Matthew 24:29 and 2 Peter 3:10–12.
Whether pictorial or literal, it describes a time of universal
terror from which there is nowhere to hide. The question
'Who can stand?' (Rev 6:17) is answered in the next chapter.

After the opening of the sixth seal, Revelation 7 provides an
interlude picturing the redeemed in heaven. God's people
are not exempt from tribulation, but are 'sealed' (7:2,4) so
that they may survive it. As the seal was an ancient mark of
ownership, so Christians are sealed with the Holy Spirit as
belonging to God (2 Cor. 1:22; Eph. 1:13).

The number 144,000 is symbolic, denoting not limitation
but completeness – probably the twelve tribes of Israel
multiplied by the twelve apostles multiplied by 1,000
(symbolising great magnitude). The tribes of Israel (which
no longer existed when John was writing) therefore
represent the whole 'Israel of God' in both Old and New
Testaments (Gal. 3:29; 6:16; Phil. 3:3), the same people
being described as 'a great multitude' in Revelation 7:9.
God knows those who are His (2 Tim. 2:19) though no
human being can count them. Their white robes show
that they have been 'washed in the blood of the Lamb'
(Rev. 7:13–14; 1 Cor. 6:11) and the remaining verses paint
a picture of the security and blessings of all God's people.

- Finally the *seventh seal* is opened (Rev. 8:1), but we are
  kept in suspense about its meaning. Just when we expect
  the vision to be completed there is a half-hour silence in
  heaven (simply a dramatic pause or a time during which
  the prayers of the saints are offered to God). We must
  wait for the end to be revealed.

Discussion Starters

1. If warfare, bloodshed, famine and death inevitably characterise the whole of human history, what role can peacemakers and aid agencies fulfil?

2. Recall briefly any stories of Christian martyrdom you know. What is the difference between Christian martyrs and suicide bombers?

3. What is the difference between 'seeking revenge' and 'being avenged' (Rev. 6:10)?

4. How far is it right, if at all, to see natural disasters (6:12ff) as judgments of God on a sinful world?

5. 'The wrath of the Lamb' (6:16) is a striking phrase. How can we reconcile the concept of wrath with the love and forgiveness we associate with the Lamb of God?

6. When and how do you think Christians are 'sealed with the Spirit'?

7. How relevant is a phrase like 'washed in the blood of the Lamb' (7:14) in an age when such language has a very old-fashioned feel to it?

8. How might the picture in Revelation 7:16–17 of an end to hunger, thirst, pain and sorrow help those undergoing great suffering today?

9. Revelation 7:17 speaks of 'springs of living water'. What other passages of Scripture can you think of which use that same picture?

10. Look again at Revelation 8:1. Why are we so uncomfortable with silence, and what is its value in our worship and discipleship?

Personal Application

At a time when many churches are in a state of decline, let the picture in these chapters of 'a great multitude that no-one could count' (Rev. 7:9) encourage us. God has His faithful people in every age and nation – let us make sure we are among them!

Yet, as today's study makes plain, being a Christian is no easy option. Jesus put it clearly: 'In this world you will have trouble. But take heart! I have overcome the world' (John 16:33). That word 'trouble' also appears in Revelation 7:14 where it is translated 'tribulation', and we are again reminded that there is a way through such difficulties for followers of the Lamb. Think for a moment of any troubles besetting you or those close to you just now, offer them to God and claim His victory to overcome them.

Seeing Jesus in the Scriptures

Today's study passage uses two contrasting pictures of Jesus: 'the wrath of the Lamb' (6:16) and 'the blood of the Lamb' (7:14). Although they may seem contradictory, both are equally true. We are familiar enough with the latter picture – Jesus shedding His blood as the Lamb of God; but He displayed His wrath (righteous anger) too in stories like the cleansing of the Temple and His denunciation of the self-righteous Pharisees. Love and judgment co-exist uniquely in Jesus, and it is supremely on the cross that (to use Graham Kendrick's phrase) 'wrath and mercy meet'. We may draw confidence from the fact that, as John Wesley said, 'The judge of all is also the saviour of all'.

WEEK 3

The Seven Trumpets

Opening Icebreaker

What musical instruments do any members of the group play? Discuss the characteristics of the various instruments and the different 'feel' they convey to their hearers. Now think particularly of the different ways in which trumpets are used and the effect they have. Apart from those mentioned in today's study, see how many other references to trumpets you can think of in the Bible.

Bible Reading

Revelation 8:2–11:19

Opening Our Eyes

Before delving into this passage we must reiterate what was said in the Introduction: namely, that the different visions in the book of Revelation describe parallel rather than consecutive events. Thus the period of time described in this vision of the seven trumpets is the same as that covered by the seven seals in our previous study, though now viewed from a different perspective.

Before the trumpets are sounded, however, we see a picture of God's people at prayer (8:3–5). Remembering that John's original readers were suffering great persecution, it is understandable that their prayers were for God's judgment on sin and injustice – and were quickly to be answered. That judgment is heralded by the sounding of trumpets, the first four of which (8:6–12) introduce calamities in the natural world. Whether John had actual events of his day in mind or not, they are certainly not unimaginable in the light of contemporary experiences of global warming, earthquakes, volcanoes, hurricanes, tsunamis, atomic bombs and nuclear fall-out.

- The *first trumpet* brings judgments on the land with fire and hail wreaking devastation.
- The *second* affects the sea, destroying ships and sea creatures.
- The *third* turns the inland springs and rivers bitter.
- The *fourth* brings the destruction of the heavens, turning light to darkness.

The fact that these disasters destroy only a third of the earth (though that is bad enough) suggests that they are warnings rather than God's final judgment. There is still time for repentance. As C.S. Lewis put it, pain is God's 'megaphone to rouse a deaf world'. The next two trumpets, however, bring stronger warnings (described as 'woes' – 8:13–9:21), this time about the work of Satan in the world.

- The *fifth trumpet* heralds the falling of a star from heaven who holds the key to the bottomless Abyss (9:1) and whose name means 'Destroyer' (9:11). Perhaps this is a picture of Satan himself, whom Jesus described in Luke 10:18 as falling 'like lightning from heaven'. Yet his power is limited; God remains in control (Rev. 9:5). The plague of locusts (reminiscent of Exodus 10:12–20) is so destructive that people long for death to escape the torment.
- The *sixth trumpet*, another 'woe' (Rev. 9:12), brings a final warning – death through warfare. If the detailed imagery of John's vision is hard to interpret, the overall meaning is clear. Though wars destroy a third of the human race, God's warning goes unheeded (9:20–21). Two thousand years later humanity has still not learnt its lesson.

Revelation 10:1–11:14 provides a break before the seventh trumpet is sounded, and describes what is happening to the Church while these judgments are taking place. A 'mighty angel' (10:1) declares that there will be no further delay before the 'mystery of God' is revealed and the gospel age is brought to completion (10:6–7). The temple in Revelation 11 symbolises the Church in the world, which remains faithful to the Word of God (described in 10:2,8–9 as a sweet-tasting scroll – cf. Ezek. 3:1–3) and fulfils in its own time the same ministry as the 'two witnesses' did in theirs (Rev. 11:3 – perhaps Moses and Elijah or the disciples sent out in twos?). Despite persecution and suppression (11:7–10), the Church is eventually revived and glorified (11:11–13).

- Finally the *seventh trumpet* ushers in the reign of Christ (11:15–19) and those who have reverenced His name are rewarded. Still we are given no details of the end, but its coming is assured.

Discussion Starters

1. What can we learn about prayer from the picture of the praying saints in Revelation 8:3–5 (cf.Psa. 141:1–2; Rom. 8:26; Heb. 7:25)?

2. What link, if any, do you think we should see between the events described in Revelation 8:6–12 and the disasters (both natural and man-made) in our own time?

3. How do you react to C.S. Lewis's description of pain as God's 'megaphone to rouse a deaf world'? Share any personal experiences of pain and suffering bringing you or others closer to God.

4. In what ways do these chapters illustrate the fact that God is still merciful, despite the woes and judgments they describe?

5. What does 'the mystery of God' mean (Rev. 10:7)?
Passages like Romans 16:25–27, Ephesians 1:9–10; 3:2–6
and 1 Corinthians 15:51 throw light on the phrase.

----

6. What does the picture of the scroll in Revelation 10:9–
11 teach us about the nature of God's Word and our
attitude to Scripture? How can it be both sweet and sour
at the same time?

----

7. What encouragement would Revelation 11:11–13 have
provided for the Church in John's day, and how far do
you think it can apply to the contemporary Church?

----

8. Can you think of historical or contemporary examples
of the Church or individuals being revived by 'a breath
of life from God' (11:11)?

Personal Application

Amid the terrible judgments in these chapters, focus on three phrases that apply to us as Christians.

- *'The prayers of all the saints'* (8:3). How much have you contributed to that great volume of prayer rising to God? However experienced we are in prayer, we are constantly challenged to deeper prayerfulness.
- *'Take the scroll ... and eat it'* (10:8–9). A prayer in the *Book of Common Prayer* speaks of the need to 'read, mark, learn and inwardly digest' the Scriptures. How much time do you give not only to reading but also to truly digesting the Bible?
- *'A breath of life from God'* (11:11). Think of times of renewal you have experienced and thank God that His Spirit continues to breathe new life whenever we are open enough to receive.

Seeing Jesus in the Scriptures

Although Jesus Himself is only mentioned once (in 11:8 referring to the crucifixion) before the final section of today's study passage, we can see Him standing in the wings and hear echoes of His words throughout it. Yet as the final trumpet is blown (11:15) there is an explosion of praise to Christ, which reflects what Paul had in mind as he wrote: 'Then the end will come, when he hands over the kingdom to God the Father after he has destroyed all dominion, authority and power. For he must reign until he has put all his enemies under his feet' (1 Cor. 15:24–25). Handel's *Messiah* wonderfully captured this scene in the 'Hallelujah Chorus'. You may like to listen to it as a fitting way of ending this session.

WEEK 4

The Seven Symbols

Opening Icebreaker

Describe and discuss some of the different symbols you have seen in the course of today. How important is symbolism in our daily lives? How many symbols can you think of that are used in Scripture to describe the devil?

Bible Reading

Revelation 12:1–14:20

Opening Our Eyes

So far John's visions have described what was happening to God's people but not why. Now we discover the answer: Satan is at war with God! This section again covers the same events as earlier ones, but now exposing the spiritual realities behind them through seven symbolic pictures.

- The *dragon* is clearly Satan (12:9) and 12:3 shows his power over the world. He once he had a place in heaven, but no longer (12:7–9)! His power is confined to the earth – 1 John 5:19 reminds us that the world is under his control.
- The male *child* (Rev. 12:5) represents Christ. John says nothing about His life and ministry, being concerned here only to assert that He completed His work and ascended into heaven. Satan's attempt to destroy Jesus (12:4) fails miserably. The Lamb wins!
- The meaning of the *woman* (12:1–2) is less clear. The fact that she gives birth to the Messiah might suggest Mary, but the context (12:13–17) makes that unlikely. Rather this is a picture of the people of God – both the old and new Israel. Having failed to destroy her child, Satan turns to attacking the woman herself (12:13), then her 'offspring' (12:17) – individual Christians. John's readers now realise that their hardships come from Satan himself.

But the plot thickens! Facing the devil is bad enough, but he has powerful allies. Revelation 13 vividly describes the fourth and fifth symbols:

- The *beast from the sea* (13:1–10) initially symbolised the Roman Empire, but typifies all anti-Christian governments. Christians in every age experience times when they must resist the state because they have 'another king, one called Jesus' (Acts 17:7 – cf.Acts 4:18–20).

- The *beast from the earth* (Rev. 13:11–18) looks like a lamb but speaks like a dragon! Jesus warned of 'wolves in sheep's clothing' (Matt. 7:15), and this beast represents false religion in its many forms – especially when too closely allied to the state (Rev. 13:12). John's readers would recognise the cult of emperor-worship here, but Christians in every age have faced battles against the deceptiveness of apparently harmless non-Christian beliefs and practices. Any religion or form of spirituality that does not acknowledge Jesus as Lord worships the beast (1 Cor. 12:3).

All who come under the influence of these beasts receive a mark (Rev. 13:16) – perhaps an allusion to owners branding their animals and slaves. All who are not sealed as belonging to Christ (7:3; 14:1) belong to Satan. The number of the beast is 666 (13:18). Since seven is the perfect number, 666 represents recurring failure – a description that is true of people too. The best of human effort cannot achieve salvation.

Two further symbols remain:

- *The Lamb and His followers* (14:1–5). Christ is worshipped by 144,000 believers (the whole Church), previously sealed on earth (7:4) but now in heaven. Not one is missing; all enjoy the blessedness of those who die in the Lord (14:13). Meanwhile on earth three angels are at work, the first (14:6–7) proclaiming the gospel as the only way to escape judgment; the second (14:8) declaring the downfall of paganism; and the third (14:9–11) the punishment of the wicked.
- *The harvest of the earth* (14:14–20). Previous visions stopped short of providing any detail about the final judgment, but now its grim reality is described in pictures reminiscent of both the Old Testament (Isa. 63:3; Joel 3:13) and the teaching of Jesus (Matt. 13:30,40–42).

evement
t. Do you
nyway?

_____

_____

destroy
his refers
ek to

_____

_____

ad in your
s of the

_____

_____

emporary
her human
you ever

_____

5. If the 'b
anti-Chr
'politics
not to l

——————
——————

6. In the l
about tl
attitude
spiritual

——————
——————

7. Is Revei
celibate:
actually

——————
——————

8. The wo
funeral
of deatl

——————
——————

9. Do you
than the

——————
——————

Personal Application

The emphasis on the power of evil in today's study could obscure the fact that Satan is a defeated enemy. We can live victoriously in the secret of Revelation 12:11, overcoming Satan only 'by the blood of the Lamb' – 'trusting Jesus every day'. If we make what He has done for us our own testimony we need fear neither the devil nor death. As Paul reminds us, 'to live is Christ and to die is gain' (Phil 1:21). Other verses here urge us to 'follow the Lamb wherever he goes' (Rev. 14:4), to 'fear God and give him glory' (14:7) and to 'obey God's commandments and remain faithful to Jesus' (14:12). Twice we are reminded that this calls for 'patient endurance' (13:10; 14:12). It is no easy calling – but it's the way to victory!

Seeing Jesus in the Scriptures

Although the authority of Christ is mentioned only once in Revelation (12:10), it is a theme frequently taken up elsewhere in the New Testament. When Jesus spoke it was always with authority (Matt. 7:29; Mark 1:27), not like the scribes, for He spoke for the Father (John 8:28; 14:10). Yet after His death and resurrection He assumed even greater authority. Having defeated Satan, He was able to assert: 'All authority in heaven and on earth has been given to me' (Matt. 28:18). How sad that He had to challenge some with the question, 'Why do you call me "Lord, Lord," and do not do what I say?' (Luke 6:46). They acknowledged His authority in theory, but it made no practical difference to their lives.

WEEK 5

The Seven Bowls

Opening Icebreaker

Have a selection of daily and local newspapers available and encourage the group to find and share any reports from them that they think typify human rebellion against God. Look especially for any in which you don't feel that the punishment fits the crime.

Bible Reading

Revelation 15:1–16:21

ing and
sions. If
y things
ave
God's
nemies
visions
ent: here
of the
l.

eaven
escribed
15:3), both
g seen as
s died the
t. 27:51;
ened to all
or those
angels
ment,
like the
gues in
ets brought
gment this
harsh or
it the ways
5:3–4).

pon the

on

ews feared)

- The *thir*
  again is
- The *fou*
  earth's i

Yet people
rather than
refusing to

- The *fiftl*
  godless
  will, like
  end in c
- The *sixtl*
  of evil (
  east) gat
  the drag
  governm
  the beas
  return o
  2 Pet. 3
  when co
  destroye
  Haifa, th
  and thei
  about th
  of Israel
  symbolic
  battlefiel
- Finally,
  complet
  the abo
  earthqua
  is done!
  the triun
  finished

Discussion Starters

1. Both the story of the Israelites crossing the Red Sea in Exodus 14 and the picture of God's victorious people in Revelation 15:2 feature 'a sea'. In what other ways might these two passages be linked?

2. Are we meant to see 'the song of Moses' and 'the song of the Lamb' (15:3) as two different songs or as one and the same – and why?

3. Scripture often exhorts us (as in Rev. 15:4) to 'fear God'. What does that really mean?

4. Commenting on Revelation 16:2 William Hendriksen writes: 'For believers in Christ the afflictions of the flesh are never bowls of wrath (cf.Rom. 8:28)'. How does that relate to your own and others' experience of physical suffering?

5. How do you account for the fact that even after so many warnings humanity does not repent of its rebellion against God (Rev. 16:9,11)?

6. How can we tell the difference between demonic 'miraculous signs' (16:14) and signs that are genuine manifestations of the Holy Spirit?

7. Revelation 16:15 describes the return of Christ. What practical difference to our lives does belief in the second coming actually make?

8. The picture of the Battle of Armageddon, however we interpret it, reminds us that the Christian life is one of continuous as well as ultimate spiritual warfare. In what ways should we take this truth more seriously in our daily lives?

Personal Application

This passage has two important themes for our discipleship. The first is *Christian worship*: as we hear the redeemed in heaven singing God's praise (15:3–4) we are reminded of our primary responsibility to 'worship God and enjoy Him for ever' (*Westminster Catechism*). We worship God because of His nature (holy, righteous, almighty) and His deeds (great and marvellous). Keeping those things in mind helps us worship Him aright, not only with our lips but with our lives.

The second theme is *Christian holiness*: the reminder to stay awake and keep our clothes with us (16:15) may seem strange, but clothes in Scripture often symbolise righteousness. Paul urges us to 'put off the old self' (Eph. 4:22) and to be 'clothed with Christ' (see Gal. 3:27). Watchfulness and holiness must go together.

Seeing Jesus in the Scriptures

Specific mention of Jesus is strangely absent from these two chapters. Nevertheless the 'song of the Lamb' is being sung, and that is a reminder that the achievements of Christ, the Lamb of God, lie behind both the victory of God and His people and the defeat of Satan being described here. Christ's finished work on the cross prepared the way for the preaching of the gospel to all nations (Rev. 15:4 – cf.Matt. 28:19), the selfless sacrifice of the saints and martyrs (Rev. 16:6 – cf.Acts 7:54–60; 12:2; Heb. 11:32–38) and the ultimate destruction of that already defeated enemy, Satan himself (Rev.16:17 – cf. Matt. 25:41; 1 John 3:8). No wonder Paul shouted 'Thanks be to God! He gives us the victory through our Lord Jesus Christ' (1 Cor. 15:57).

WEEK 6

Final Judgment and the Triumph of God

Opening Icebreaker

Imagine you have been invited to a wedding. How would you set about deciding what to wear? Would you ever consider going in borrowed clothes? Why do you think John uses the picture of a wedding to describe the time when God's people are finally united with their Lord?

Bible Reading

Revelation 17:1–20:15

Opening Our Eyes

Unlike previous sections, this long section is mostly concerned with the future. We can study it only in broad brush strokes, looking first at four pictures of the day of judgment:

The fall of Babylon
Since Babylon was destroyed before John's vision, the name (Rev. 17:5; 18:2,21) cannot refer to the actual city. Initially it described degenerate Rome and her successive emperors (17:7–14). But more widely 'Babylon' symbolises godless society everywhere. It is personified as a prostitute: although men and women were created to become 'the Bride of Christ' (see 19:7) they have been unfaithful, seduced by temptation and intoxicated by worldly pleasures (17:2). The prostitute sits on a scarlet beast (17:3), for satanic power motivates her. Yet her days are numbered and Revelation 18 graphically describes her fall, ending with a grim picture of silence, darkness and desolation. Those with vested interests in corrupt power (18:9–10), selfish materialism (18:11–17) and sea-going profiteering (18:17–19) bemoan their loss. While most lament Babylon's downfall, the Church triumphant rejoices in it (19:1–5). This is no vindictive delight in the sufferings of others but a celebration of divine justice. Right has finally triumphed!

The destruction of the beasts
The two beasts of Revelation 13 (anti-Christian government and false religion) reappear (19:17–21) and the entire unbelieving world gathers for the final conflict. The beasts are seized and destroyed. Satan's allies have gone; only he remains.

The overthrow of Satan
Revelation 20 introduces 'the millennium' (20:2–3,7). Some (pre-millennialists) see this as a period of 1,000 years following the return of Christ; others (post-millennialists) as

a final period during which Satan's influence is restricted after which Christ will return; yet others (a-millennialists) as symbolising the whole gospel age between the first and second comings of Christ. The 'binding' of Satan began with the incarnation of Jesus; although still alive and well, Satan is restrained and cannot prevent the spread of the gospel to every nation. Things may be bad but would have been unimaginably worse if Christ had never come!

Yet at the end of the gospel age Satan is 'released' (20:7) before his ultimate overthrow. We are not told why, nor given any further explanation. Sufficient only to know that, in Luther's words, 'his doom is writ'!

The judgment of the dead
As Paul teaches, 'we will all stand before God's judgment seat' (Rom. 14:10; 2 Cor. 5:10). That moment has now come (Rev. 20:11–15). We all determine our own destiny. Those who trust Jesus as Lord are inscribed in the book of life and the rest, their deeds recorded elsewhere, receive the just consequences of their choice. All who follow Satan share his fate. Although judgment dominates this section, two passages describe the final triumph of God and His people:

The marriage of the Lamb
In this heavenly marriage Christ Himself is the Bridegroom and His Church is the Bride (19:7), now finally united with her Lord. Her beautiful clean wedding clothes, righteous deeds, are a gift from the Bridegroom whose own robe displays the marks of sacrifice (19:13). As Charles Wesley put it: 'Alive in Him, my living Head, and clothed in righteousness divine.'

The rider on the white horse
Jesus is now seen as a horseman variously called 'Faithful and True' (19:11), 'Word of God' (19:13) and 'King of kings and Lord of lords' (19:16). It is this majestic picture of the risen and glorified Lord that governs the rest of the book.

Discussion Starters

1. What other cities besides Babylon does Scripture use to symbolise wickedness? If John had been writing today can you suggest a modern city he might have used instead of Babylon?

2. In what ways do people today become 'intoxicated by worldly pleasures' (see Rev. 17:2)? Why do you think John used the word 'intoxicated'?

3. Some people find the idea of rejoicing at the downfall of the wicked repugnant (19:1–5). How would you respond to such an objection?

4. What do you see as the pros and cons of the different interpretations of the millennium (Rev. 20), and does it really matter which view we adopt?

5. What biblical and other evidence is there to support the assertion that Satan is 'bound' and his influence in the world restricted (20:2), and how does this truth help us in our own struggle against sin?

6. If salvation is by grace through faith rather than through our own good works, why does Revelation 20:13 say that we will be judged according to what we have done?

_____

_____

7. Revelation 19 includes the longest collection of hymns in the whole of the book of Revelation. How important are hymns in Christian worship, and what purpose do they fulfil?

_____

_____

8. How far do you think that what we wear expresses who we are? Can you think of other passages besides Revelation 19:7–8 that use the analogy of clothing to describe character?

_____

_____

9. In what ways do the three names given to Jesus in Revelation 19:11–16 reflect what we learn about Him from other parts of the New Testament? What other names of Jesus can you think of, and what does it mean to do things 'in His name'?

_____

_____

Personal Application

Those who share the victory of the Lamb are described as 'called, chosen and faithful followers' (Rev. 17:14) – a reminder of both the privilege and the responsibility of Christians. Faithfulness is relatively easy when things are going well, but the real test comes when, like these early Christians, we have to face opposition and hardship. Pray that you will be able to 'hold to the testimony of Jesus' (19:10).

One practical aid to faithfulness comes in the call to God's people, whenever tempted to involvement with the sins of the world ('Babylon'), to 'come out of her' (18:4). Consider Paul's advice on this topic in 2 Corinthians 6:14–18 and Jesus' teaching about being in the world but not of it (John 17:13–19), and ask yourself whether you are involved in worldly compromises you need to leave behind.

Seeing Jesus in the Scriptures

Two main descriptions of Jesus in this section offer widely contrasting pictures: the Lamb at His wedding feast (Rev. 19:6–10) and the horseman in a blood-soaked robe leading His armies in victory (19:11–16). Both reflect teaching about Jesus in other parts of the Bible – as the 'Lamb of God' in John 1:29; and as the bringer of victory in Romans 8:37 and 1 Corinthians 15:57, to cite just two instances. Yet for all their contrast these two pictures merge into one when we realise that the blood on the horseman's robe is the same as that shed by the crucified Lamb of God; both are pictures of sacrifice and both depict ultimate victory, underlining the theme of this book – the Lamb wins!

WEEK 7

All Things New

Opening Icebreaker

Has anyone in the group had anything brand new this
week? Was it a necessity or just a matter of wanting to
treat yourself? By contrast, has anyone had anything old
restored and renovated so that it is as good as new? What
are the pros and cons of replacement versus renewal?

Bible Reading

Revelation 21:1–22:21

Opening Our Eyes

After the dramatic and violent pictures of previous chapters we now change mood and discover the nearest thing Scripture provides to a picture of heaven. Revelation 21 begins with the key word 'new' (21:1–5) – the Greek means 'totally transformed' rather than 'recently made'. Earlier chapters described a *new name* (2:17) and a *new song* (5:9) for God's people; now John describes a *new heaven and a new earth*. If we compare the first and last books of the Bible, Genesis described the creation of heaven and earth; Revelation sees it totally renewed. In the beginning the sun and moon gave light to the world; now the Lamb provides all the light needed (21:23). In Eden stood the forbidden tree; in the new Jerusalem stands the tree of life (22:14). In Genesis humanity was banished from paradise; here paradise is restored. Truly everything is made new!

Two major pictures dominate these closing chapters:

The Holy City

Jerusalem was one of the wonders of antiquity and its Temple was a particularly striking sight. Yet it cannot compare with the 'new Jerusalem' (21:2,10), the 'Holy City', which John portrays in vivid pictures. Its foundations and gates indicate that God's faithful people in both Old and New Testaments are one (21:12–14); its entrances provide access from every corner of the world (21:13 – cf.5:9; 7:9); its vastness can accommodate all God's people (21:15–17); and its shape (a perfect cube – 21:16) reflects that of the Holy of Holies – truly 'God himself will be with them' (21:3). What a picture of absolute security for all in Christ!

Two characteristics of this Holy City emerge. First, it is *a place of beauty* (21:18–21). We need not press the significance of individual precious stones but the overall impression is breathtaking, its glory reflecting God Himself (21:11). Second, it is *a place of purity* (21:27). There is neither sea (21:1) nor curse (22:3) nor darkness (22:5) – all symbols of evil – and death, mourning, crying and pain (characteristics of our present life in a fallen world) are no more (21:4). The river of life flowing through the city brings healing and fruitfulness, and the Lamb rules over all (22:1–2). What a prospect!

The heavenly Bride

This picture of the Church in our last study (19:7) recurs here (21:1–9). Both passages emphasise the Bride being 'prepared', a reminder that the Church is betrothed to Christ and her task (yours and mine) is constantly to be getting ready for that great day. But how? The same two characteristics emerge as in the Holy City: beauty and purity. Even the plainest of brides looks beautiful in her wedding dress! So too the *beauty* of the Bride of Christ lies in her 'dress', Christian character (21:2 – cf.19:7–8). The need for *purity* too (21:8 – cf.Eph. 5:27) challenges us to holiness and chastity in a society that often rejects biblical standards of Christian behaviour.

As John ends his book he reminds his readers – then and now – that what he has written is nothing less than the word of God (22:18–19) and is to be obeyed (22:7) and proclaimed (22:10). There is still time to turn to Christ and find life (22:14,17), but it is short. Christ is coming soon (22:7,12,20). His work is complete and His victory sure. Satan and his allies have done their worst – but at the end of human history the Lamb wins!

Discussion Starters

1. What other examples of the use of the word 'new' can you think of besides those in the book of Revelation? In the light of these, why do you think Christians are often so resistant to change?

   _____

   _____

2. What do you imagine heaven to be like? Share what you find either helpful or puzzling about the pictures of heaven in the final two chapters of Revelation.

   _____

   _____

3. What do you think Jesus meant by the claim 'I am the Alpha and the Omega, the First and the Last, the Beginning and the End' (Rev. 21:6; 22:13)?

   _____

   _____

4. Someone has said, 'The ugliness in the world is a result of the Fall.' Do you agree? What implications does the emphasis on beauty in these chapters have for our church buildings, our worship and our discipleship?

   _____

   _____

5. How can we ensure that our names are 'written in the Lamb's book of life'?

   _____

   _____

6. Nuns often wear a ring on their wedding finger as a symbol that they are 'married' to Christ. What other material reminders of our relationship to Christ have you come across, and how helpful do you find such things?

_____

_____

7. In what different ways is 'the Lamb' mentioned in these two chapters, and what do those different references say about who He is or what He does?

_____

_____

8. What would John's picture of the river of life in Revelation 22:1–2 have meant to his first readers living in a Mediterranean climate? What other uses of the symbol of a river can you think of elsewhere in the Bible?

_____

_____

9. How realistic is it to expect twenty-first-century Christians to live up to the standards of sexual behaviour taught in the Bible?

_____

_____

10. In the light of the teaching of the book of Revelation, how true is it to say that 'history is really His story'?

_____

_____

Personal Application

The picture of Christians as 'the Bride of Christ' is both encouraging and demanding. 'Betrothal' in Scripture was regarded as binding, requiring absolute faithfulness of both parties – hence the stress on purity in these chapters. Reflect for a moment on how faithful you have been to Christ, and any areas of your life where purity remains an unachieved aim. Think too of the time, money and energy a bride puts into preparing for her wedding day, and ask yourself how much effort you put into making your life (like Mother Teresa's) 'something beautiful for God'. The vision of who we really are (the 'fiancée' of Christ) should both challenge and inspire us to prepare ourselves for what we are to become (the 'wife' of the King of kings).

Seeing Jesus in the Scriptures

The words 'I am the Alpha and the Omega' come twice in these final chapters of the book of Revelation (21:6; 22:13) and provide a fitting reminder that Jesus Christ strides across the pages not just of the New Testament but the Old as well. As He told His companions walking to Emmaus, there are things said about Him 'in all the Scriptures' (Luke 24:27), and He is the key to understanding not this book only but the Bible as a whole. Jesus was active in creation when the world began (John 1:1–3,10); Jesus has continued to uphold all things by His powerful word (Heb. 1:3); and Jesus is the One who will bring history to its close. No wonder John ended this book with the prayer, 'Come, Lord Jesus.'

Leader's Notes

Tackling 19 chapters of Revelation in only seven studies is a daunting task, and detailed examination of every verse is clearly not possible. Our aim therefore is to help group members towards an overview of the main themes and encourage them to explore them further on their own.

At the first meeting you may want to read the Bible passage in its entirety, but since this will take up quite a bit of group time it would be helpful in subsequent weeks if people could read the suggested passage at home before coming to the group.

It may not be possible to use all the discussion starters provided for these sessions, and leaders should select those most appropriate for their group.

Week 1: The Lamb upon the Throne

Opening Icebreaker
At this first meeting allow time for people to talk freely around the suggested topics, which are intended to put them at ease and offer a non-threatening and enjoyable way of getting them used to contributing to the group. The discussion should then be linked into the Bible passage describing the throne room of heaven.

Aim of the Session
The main aim in this first session is to catch a glimpse of the judgment throne of the triumphant Lamb of God and to enter into the worship offered to Him. He is dominant in this and each succeeding vision. The word 'worship' comes from the Anglo-Saxon 'worth-ship'; note how often the word 'worthy' occurs here.

Discussion starters 1, 4, 6 and 8: These questions are designed to enable everyone to join in and express their own views – especially important at this first meeting. There are not necessarily 'right' and 'wrong' answers; the aim is to help people to make links between what they read here and their personal discipleship and corporate church life, while exploring some of the verses in these chapters in rather greater detail.

Discussion starter 2: Again we link Scripture and experience, but this time going rather deeper. This question gives opportunity for people to share something of their personal spiritual experience, as well as opening others up to the possibility of experiencing the Spirit in their lives. Note that being 'in the Spirit' can mean both the normal experience of believers indwelt by the Holy Spirit or (as in this case) a more unusual trance-like vision given by the Spirit on special occasions for special purposes (see also Ezek. 3:12,14; Acts 10:9–16; 16:6–10; Rev. 1:10).

Discussion starter 3: Bring out the fact that the rainbow is the sign of God's promise and that His Word is always trustworthy and reliable.

Discussion starter 5: This question acknowledges the fact that there are different interpretations of these (and many other) passages, and gives opportunity for these to be aired by any in the group who may already have studied Revelation more deeply. Gently suppress any dogmatism – nobody can be certain that theirs is the 'right' interpretation!

Discussion starter 7: This question is intended to draw out the fact that the desire to dispense with hymns and songs written a long time ago is too simplistic. Even very old hymns can become 'new songs' when we experience the truths they describe for the first time.

Discussion starter 9: This is a simple question, but not an easy one! Try to avoid sentimentalism, but in an age when green issues are rightly being given greater prominence it reminds us that 'the earth is the LORD's and everything in it' (Psa. 24:1).

Week 2: The Seven Seals

Opening Icebreaker

This exercise introduces the concept of things being sealed and difficult to open, the theme of today's passage. The discussion about the purpose of a seal should lead into the idea that it secures the contents so that no one but the person for whom it is intended has the right to open it.

Aim of the Session

Since Revelation consists of parallel visions rather than consecutive pictures, it is important to establish that understanding in this session. Succeeding weeks will cover the same period of human history, though using different symbolism. Today's passage introduces an example of the numerical symbolism of this book: as a general guide 'three' symbolises heaven, 'four' the earth, 'seven' perfection, 'ten' magnitude and 'twelve' the Church (hence 144,000 stands for the Church which cannot be numbered).

Discussion starter 1: Avoid undue pessimism about our human situation; focus on the fact that it is worth working for such relief and reconciliation as we can achieve, however imperfect it may be.

Discussion starter 2: The difference here is one of motivation. Suicide bombers seek to destroy themselves and others to achieve their own ends; Christian martyrs are prepared to face death (though they do not actively seek it) out of faithfulness to Christ, but never seek hurt for others.

Discussion starter 3: Scripture teaches us not to seek personal revenge but to leave things in God's hands. A helpful passage on this topic is Romans 12:17–21.

Discussion starter 4: This question raises all manner of philosophical difficulties! The aim here, however, is to understand that while many natural disasters are simply the result of being on a living planet, others can be traced directly to the greed and sin of humankind (deforestation and global warming, for example). We need to live responsibly in God's world.

Discussion starter 5: It is important not to define 'love' too sentimentally. Love and justice are two sides of the same coin (Psa. 33:5). Perhaps the human analogy of parents sometimes having to punish their children might help. Remember too that Jesus displayed righteous anger at the sin of the moneychangers in the Temple (Matt. 21:12–13).

Discussion starter 6: The New Testament teaches that Christ gives us the gift of His Spirit when we first believe in Him. Look at the passages referred to in 'Opening our Eyes' (Eph. 1:13 and 2 Cor. 1:22). Subsequent experiences of the Holy Spirit need to be described in other terms.

Discussion starter 7: The point here is to encourage the group not only to grasp the fact that our cleansing from sin results only from the death of Jesus on the cross, but also to recognise the need to express that truth in language that contemporary non-Christians will understand.

Discussion starter 8: The prospect of an end to suffering beyond the grave will be an encouragement to some – particularly those nearing the end of their earthly life;

but remember also the concern of Jesus and the apostles for people's physical needs in this life and how Christians through the centuries have been at the forefront of the relief of hunger and suffering.

Discussion starter 9: This question gives an opportunity to share such Bible knowledge as the group may have. If help is needed, look at passages such as Psalm 23:2, Isaiah 58:11, John 4:14, 7:37–38.

Discussion starter 10: Some Christian traditions are more accustomed to silence in their worship and the practice of Christian meditation than others. Explore this question as objectively as possible and encourage people to be open to things that may come from beyond their own tradition.

Week 3: The Seven Trumpets

Opening Icebreaker
Everyone should be able to contribute to this discussion whether they are musicians or not. Historically, trumpets have been used for fanfares on ceremonial occasions and to rally troops in battle. Their piercing sound carries long distances and they engender a sense of excitement and anticipation. Other references to trumpets in Scripture include Exodus 19:16–19, Joshua 6:1–20, 1 Corinthians 14:8; 15:52 and 1 Thessalonians 4:16.

Aim of the Session
In this long section we again see human history under God's judgment, though we are reminded that Satan is himself a fallen angel and cannot ultimately harm those who belong to Christ. The Church may go through periods of hardship and decline, but God is still in control and the Lamb is on the throne.

Discussion starter 1: The main lesson here is that God does hear and answer prayer and that there is special power in the united prayers of His people. The 'incense' may refer to the prayers of Christ on our behalf (Heb. 7:25) and the help of the Spirit in our praying (Rom. 8:26).

Discussion starter 2: These pictures of fire, drought, disasters at sea and pollution on the land are all familiar to us. The group will no doubt have different views on how far they are to be seen as direct judgments of God. Again, the distinction needs to be made between purely natural disasters and those resulting from human activity.

Discussion starter 3: This question provides opportunity for members of the group to share from their own experience. The sad truth is that while suffering does bring many closer to God (and this should be true for Christians – 1 Pet. 4:12–19), others blame God for it and harden their hearts against Him.

Discussion starter 4: Note the fact that these judgments affect only a third of the world (Rev. 8:7–12; 9:15) and that despite their ferocity God does not allow them to bring ultimate destruction (9:5). 2 Peter 3:9 throws light on this passage.

Discussion starter 5: The word 'mystery' in the New Testament means not an unsolvable puzzle but something kept hidden until the right time comes for it to be revealed. Thus the gospel was kept hidden until the coming of Christ, and Paul revealed to the Corinthians what will happen at the resurrection of the dead. There is much about the future that we do not understand at present, but the time will come when it all becomes clear. We must resist the temptation to imagine that we already have all the answers.

Discussion starter 6: Scripture is given to us by God (2 Tim. 3:16) to be 'inwardly digested' and then proclaimed to others. Yet God's Word has different effects on different people (see 1 Cor. 1:18). Sharing the gospel can be a difficult burden to bear when others reject it, and though the gospel itself is sweet it can leave a bitter taste when that happens.

Discussion starter 7: The persecuted Christians of John's day could have been forgiven for thinking that the Church might not survive, and this passage showed them that God could renew and empower His people and they would overcome. The Church militant on earth would become the Church triumphant in heaven. Today's Church is often pessimistic about its future, but Scripture reminds us that God has not finished with us yet. Our future is secure.

Discussion starter 8: This provides an opportunity for recalling stories of revival in the history of the Church as well as sharing testimony about experiences of personal renewal.

Week 4: The Seven Symbols

Opening Icebreaker
Symbols seen might include road signs, trademarks, disabled signs, flags, badges, signs on domestic appliances, etc. Few parts of our lives are unaffected by symbolism. Pictures of the devil include a serpent (Gen. 3), tempter (Matt. 4), prince of demons (Matt. 12:24), murderer and liar (John 8:44), angel of light (2 Cor. 11:14), trapper (2 Tim. 2:26), holder of the power of death (Heb. 2:14), roaring lion (1 Peter 5:8), red dragon (Rev. 12:3) and accuser (Rev. 12:10).

Aim of the Session
Today's passage helped its first readers to see their

persecution as part of the wider conflict between Satan and the purposes of God. That understanding is the main aim of today's study. Satan's influence is great, but he is a defeated enemy. Christians can live victoriously through Christ.

Discussion starter 1: This introduces discussion about the reality of the devil and the need to understand his strategy. Both Jesus and Paul took him seriously, and so should we. This is not to evade responsibility for our own sin, but to recognise that we are engaged in constant spiritual warfare (Eph. 6:10–18).

Discussion starter 2: This incident refers to Herod's slaughter of the innocents (Matt. 2:16). Other occasions were the storm on the lake (Mark 4:37–41) and the cross itself (Luke 23:18ff). The temptations were perhaps a further attempt (Luke 4:1–12).

Discussion starter 3: Another opportunity to share personal experience and testimony.

Discussion starter 4: Examples include well-known people (Dietrich Bonhoeffer resisting the Nazis, Archbishop Luwum opposing Idi Amin, Martin Luther King fighting racism) as well as unknown Christians in places such as Eastern Europe, the Middle East and China – not to mention contemporary Britain.

Discussion starter 5: Distinguish between politics as a necessary system of government and the corrupt abuse of political power. We need more Christians in politics, not fewer, and should support those who serve in that way in our prayers (1 Tim. 2:1–2). Ultimately, however, our hope is in Christ, not politics.

Discussion starter 6: Contemporary interest in spirituality should be recognised as an expression of the fact that we are created in God's image and have an inbuilt inclination to seek after spiritual reality. However, spirituality in itself is insufficient and Christians should use this interest as an opportunity to direct people towards the truth as it is in Jesus.

Discussion starter 7: This question helps us to wrestle with the meaning of the text. The Bible never sees sexual relationships as wrong in themselves. Some Christians, particularly in the monastic tradition, have chosen celibacy but it is never required of all. This verse more probably refers to spiritual and moral purity rather than sexual chastity, underlining the need for Christians not to compromise with worldly standards or behaviour.

Discussion starter 8: This question gives an opportunity to share feelings honestly. Many fear the process of dying and the fact that death separates us from loved ones on earth, rather than what lies beyond the grave. Try to capture the confidence and hope of the Christian teaching about death summed up so wonderfully in Paul's words, 'For me to live is Christ and to die is gain' (Phil. 1:21).

Discussion starter 9: Answers to this question will vary according to the experience of group. Some preachers may over-emphasise this topic, while others ignore it completely. We simply need to be faithful to the teaching of Scripture as a whole, recognising that the good news makes sense only in the context of the bad news about sin, judgment and their eternal consequences.

Week 5: The Seven Bowls

Opening Icebreaker
This exercise is designed to introduce the subject of punishment for wrongdoing, and the need for justice to be done. It will hopefully show that human sin is ultimately not only an offence against other people but also against God Himself.

Aim of the Session
This section again describes the punishment of the wicked, and our aim is to help group members see that for God to punish evildoers is a fitting response to what they have done and a legitimate expression of His truth and justice. Good and evil cannot coexist in the world forever without one or the other emerging victorious – and the outcome of this battle is never in doubt.

Discussion starter 1: Both passages are celebrating deliverance and freedom, from the Egyptians and from the power of Satan respectively. In both instances it is God who is the deliverer, and both experiences result in a spontaneous outburst of song.

Discussion starter 2: Although the words are different in Old and New Testaments, and in that sense they are two different songs, the theme and the subject are the same. Neither song celebrates human achievement; both celebrate the deliverance brought about by the hand of God. As such they may be seen as a single song glorying in the redemptive activity of God across the centuries.

Discussion starter 3: Clearly we are not to be 'frightened' of God – unless we decide to rebel against Him (Luke 12:5). Passages such as Deuteronomy 10:12, Philippians 2:12, 2 Timothy 1:7 and 1 John 4:18 help to throw light on its true meaning. A better translation might be 'revere' or 'be in awe of'.

Discussion starter 4: Encourage the group to share their own experiences of serious illness or other forms of physical suffering, and how they related it to their faith. Hendriksen's point is that for Christians these experiences are not to be seen as divine punishment but as part of that whole tapestry of life (both joy and pain) through which God works for our ultimate good. See also 2 Corinthians 1:3–11 and 12:7–10.

Discussion starter 5: The story of human rebellion against God began in the Garden of Eden and has continued ever since. Those whose eyes have been opened to the truth of the gospel find it difficult to understand why others cannot or will not see it, but this is further evidence of the influence of Satan in the world – a major theme of the book of Revelation. See also 1 Corinthians 2:14 and 2 Corinthians 4:3–4.

Discussion starter 6: Encourage the group to share any experiences of 'miraculous signs' they may have had. Scripture's direct answer to the question of how to distinguish between demonic and spiritual signs is found in 1 John 4:1–3 (cf.Deut. 18:10–12; Matt. 24:24).

Discussion starter 7: The return of Christ concentrates our minds on our behaviour and lifestyle. We should live constantly in the light of His coming (see 1 Thess. 5:4–8; 2 Pet. 3:10–14).

Discussion starter 8: We need to be aware that the devil will constantly seek to ensnare us and divert us from our desire to follow Christ (1 Pet. 5:8). Often temptation comes when we least expect it. The classic passage on spiritual warfare is Ephesians 6:10–18.

Week 6: Final Judgment and the Triumph of God

Opening Icebreaker

Share wedding experiences before linking into the theme of the 'wedding of the Lamb' (Rev. 19:7). The analogy of marriage is used in the Old Testament (especially Hosea), by John the Baptist (John 3:29), in the teaching of Jesus (Mark 2:19–20, and Matt. 22:1–14), and in Ephesians 5:22–32. Ideally, a wedding marks the consummation of a loving relationship and the establishing of a permanent and joyful union (1 Thess. 4:17).

Aim of the Session

Today's aim is to see that, however strong the powers of evil, they will not have the last word. Satan will finally be destroyed. Difficult though the Christian life is, it ends in ultimate victory and everlasting joy.

Discussion starter 1: Include Sodom, Gomorrah, Nineveh and Corinth. Modern cities might include Bangkok, Las Vegas and Soho – though don't take this part too seriously!

Discussion starter 2: 'Intoxicated' signifies being enticed and stimulated by something that causes a loss of clear thinking and self-control – not only alcohol but many other things (even some not necessarily bad in themselves).

Discussion starter 3: It is important for any who find this a problem to air their feelings. The rejoicing described is more a response to the victory of God than to the destruction of those who opposed Him. Justice demands that for righteousness to be upheld wrong must be punished. We can trust God to do what is right (Gen. 18:25).

Discussion starter 4: Avoid this question if it is not appropriate for your group. The 'pre-millennialist' view sees Revelation as a sort of future time-chart, though it does take its message for today seriously. 'Post-millennialists' take a more optimistic (some say over-optimistic) view of the future, looking for a period of unprecedented spiritual advance before the end. The 'a-millennialist' sees Revelation as more symbolic than literal, though some feel they thereby make its message less sharp than it should be. Since truth is important it does matter which view we take, but in terms of everyday practical Christian living the fact of Christ's return is more important than the timing or sequence of events.

Discussion starter 5: Jesus' parable in Mark 3:23–27 speaks of the binding of Satan. We see evidence of the restriction of his power in the wilderness temptations, his 'fall' witnessed by the disciples (Luke 10:18), his defeat through the death and resurrection of Jesus and the ongoing spread of the gospel from New Testament times onwards. Although we continue to experience temptation, Satan need not have the mastery over us (Rom. 6:11–14; 1 Cor. 10:13; 1 John 3:7–10).

Discussion starter 6: There is similar teaching in Romans 2:6 and James 2:14–18. While it is important to grasp the truth of Ephesians 2:8–9, it is equally important to recognise that Christians too will be judged (1 Cor. 3:11–15; 2 Cor. 5:10; 1 Pet. 4:17), and faith must be expressed in deeds.

Discussion starter 7: Whatever worship styles we prefer, they would be greatly impoverished without hymns and songs to exhort, teach, celebrate the mighty acts of God and express our worship. They also link Christians across the centuries as we use the words and music of earlier generations.

Discussion starter 8: Personal tastes in clothing and the use of uniforms are relevant here. The clothing analogy is also found in Romans 13:14; Ephesians 4:22–25; 6:11; Colossians 3:12–14; 1 Peter 3:3–4; 5:5.

Discussion starter 9: Suggestions here include Hebrews 3:6; John 1:1,14; 8:31–32; 14:6; 18:33–37; 20:28; Acts 2:36; Romans 10:9; Philippians 2:10–11. Members of the group will probably know many of the names of Jesus. Doing things in His name means doing them on His behalf, with His authority, for His sake and to His glory.

Week 7: All Things New

Opening Icebreaker

This icebreaker introduces the subject of newness and tries to highlight the distinction between the two Greek words for 'new' – *neos* (new in the sense of recent, young, only just made) and *kainos* (meaning new and fresh in quality, completely different, totally renewed). It is the latter word that is used in Revelation.

Aim of the Session

The aim in these final and rather more familiar chapters is to encourage us to see that Christ has indeed won the final victory and that, beyond the day of judgment, all who belong to Christ can be assured of a secure and eternal future with Him in the glory of heaven, free at last from all sorrow and sin.

Discussion starter 1: Examples include new wineskins (Matt. 9:16–17), the new commandment (John 13:34), the new tomb in which Jesus was laid (John 19:41), the cup of the new covenant (Luke 22:20), becoming a new creation (2 Cor. 5:17) and putting on the new self (Eph. 4:24). The group may well think of others, as well as having their own views on attitudes to change.

Discussion starter 2: A straightforward question encouraging people to share their own views but to root them in Revelation.

Discussion starter 3: This claim applies both to the activity of Jesus in the created world (John 1:1–3; Col. 1:17; Heb. 1:3) and in our salvation which He began through His coming, accomplished by His death and resurrection and will complete when we are taken to be with Him for ever (Heb. 12:2; 13:8). He spans the whole of human history.

Discussion starter 4: Ugliness is not to be interpreted here as only physical. Whatever people's views, bring out the influence and importance of aesthetics for our witness and worship (architecture, lighting, design and décor) and the challenge to reflect the beauty of Jesus in our lives.

Discussion starter 5: This basic question is included to help any in the group who may be unsure of their own salvation to understand that our names are recorded in 'the Lamb's book of life' only when we turn to Him in repentance and faith, receive Him into our lives as Saviour and Lord and follow Him faithfully as His disciples.

Discussion starter 6: Suggestions may include the wearing of crosses and badges, 'fish' car stickers and perhaps the carrying of a pocket Bible or other things.

Discussion starter 7: References come in Revelation 21:9,14,22,23,27 and 22:1,3. They speak respectively about Jesus as the Bridegroom who loves His Church, the Master who called the apostles, the Way to God, the Light of the world, the Saviour who gives life to His followers and the King who reigns over all.

Discussion starter 8: Hot climates especially depended on rivers for their agriculture, health, nourishment, transport and livelihood. Other 'river' symbols in Scripture include Genesis 2:10, Psalms 1:3 and 46:4, Isaiah 43:2, Ezekiel 47:1–12 and John 7:38.

Discussion starter 9: The emphasis on the purity of the Bride of Christ in Revelation may prove difficult for members of the group or their families who struggle with the biblical teaching on sexual morality in a society that has largely rejected it. We need to be sensitive and loving, yet firm and clear about what Christ expects of us in this area of our lives.

Discussion starter 10: This question gives an opportunity for the group to review the whole panorama of the book of Revelation, and to underline the fact that Christ is the central figure who dominates the story from the beginning to the end of time.

National Distributors

UK: (and countries not listed below)
CWR, Waverley Abbey House, Waverley Lane, Farnham, Surrey GU9 8EP.
Tel: (01252) 784700 Outside UK (+44) 1252 784700

AUSTRALIA: CMC Australasia, PO Box 519, Belmont, Victoria 3216.
Tel: (03) 5241 3288 Fax: (03) 5241 3290

CANADA: Cook Communications Ministries, PO Box 98, 55 Woodslee Avenue, Paris, Ontario N3L 3E5.
Tel: 1800 263 2664

GHANA: Challenge Enterprises of Ghana, PO Box 5723, Accra.
Tel: (021) 222437/223249 Fax: (021) 226227

HONG KONG: Cross Communications Ltd, 1/F, 562A Nathan Road, Kowloon.
Tel: 2780 1188 Fax: 2770 6229

INDIA: Crystal Communications, 10-3-18/4/1, East Marredpalli, Secunderabad – 500026, Andhra Pradesh.
Tel/Fax: (040) 27737145

KENYA: Keswick Books and Gifts Ltd, PO Box 10242, Nairobi.
Tel: (02) 331692/226047 Fax: (02) 728557

MALAYSIA: Salvation Book Centre (M) Sdn Bhd, 23 Jalan SS 2/64, 47300 Petaling Jaya, Selangor.
Tel: (03) 78766411/78766797 Fax: (03) 78757066/78756360

NEW ZEALAND: CMC Australasia, PO Box 36015, Lower Hutt.
Tel: 0800 449 408 Fax: 0800 449 049

NIGERIA: FBFM, Helen Baugh House, 96 St Finbarr's College Road, Akoka, Lagos.
Tel: (01) 7747429/4700218/825775/827264

PHILIPPINES: OMF Literature Inc, 776 Boni Avenue, Mandaluyong City.
Tel: (02) 531 2183 Fax: (02) 531 1960

SOUTH AFRICA: Struik Christian Books, 80 MacKenzie Street, PO Box 1144, Cape Town 8000.
Tel: (021) 462 4360 Fax: (021) 461 3612

SRI LANKA: Christombu Publications (Pvt) Ltd, Bartlett House, 65 Braybrooke Place, Colombo 2.
Tel: (9411) 2421073/2447665

TANZANIA: CLC Christian Book Centre, PO Box 1384, Mkwepu Street, Dar es Salaam.
Tel/Fax: (022) 2119439

USA: Cook Communications Ministries, PO Box 98, 55 Woodslee Avenue, Paris, Ontario N3L 3E5, Canada.
Tel: 1800 263 2664

ZIMBABWE: Word of Life Books (Pvt) Ltd, Christian Media Centre, 8 Aberdeen Road, Avondale,
PO Box A480 Avondale, Harare.
Tel: (04) 333355 or 091301188

For email addresses, visit the CWR website: www.cwr.org.uk
CWR is a registered charity – Number 294387
CWR is a limited company registered in England – Registration Number 1990308

Day and Residential Courses

Counselling Training

Leadership Development

Biblical Study Courses

Regional Seminars

Ministry to Women

Daily Devotionals

Books and Videos

Conference Centre

Trusted all Over the World

CWR HAS GAINED A WORLDWIDE reputation as a centre of excellence for Bible-based training and resources. From our headquarters at Waverley Abbey House, Farnham, England, we have been serving God's people for 40 years with a vision to help apply God's Word to everyday life and relationships. The daily devotional *Every Day with Jesus* is read by nearly a million people in more than 150 countries, and our unique courses in biblical studies and pastoral care are respected all over the world. Waverley Abbey House provides a conference centre in a tranquil setting.

For free brochures on our seminars and courses, conference facilities, or a catalogue of CWR resources, please contact us at the following address.
CWR, Waverley Abbey House, Waverley Lane, Farnham, Surrey GU9 8EP, UK

Telephone: **+44 (0)1252 784700**
Email: **mail@cwr.org.uk**
Website: **www.cwr.org.uk**

CWR Applying God's Word
to everyday life and relationships

Also available in the bestselling
Cover to Cover Bible Study Series

The Second Coming
[available May 2007]
ISBN-13: 978-1-85345-422-6
ISBN-10: 1-85345-422-2

Philippians [available May 2007]
ISBN-13: 978-1-85345-421-9
ISBN-10: 1-85345-421-4

The Prodigal
Amazing grace
ISBN-13: 978-1-85345-412-7
ISBN-10: 1-85345-412-5

Genesis 1–11
Foundations of reality
ISBN-13: 978-1-85345-404-2
ISBN-10: 1-85345-404-4

Colossians
In Christ alone
ISBN-13: 978-1-85345-405-9
ISBN-10: 1-85345-405-2

Fruit of the Spirit
Growing more like Jesus
ISBN-13: 978-1-85345-375-5
ISBN-10: 1-85345-375-7

Jeremiah
The passionate prophet
ISBN-13: 978-1-85345-372-4
ISBN-10: 1-85345-372-2

The Sermon on the Mount
Life within the new covenant
ISBN-13: 978-1-85345-370-0
ISBN-10: 1-85345-370-6

Proverbs
Living a life of wisdom
ISBN-13: 978-1-85345-373-1
ISBN-10: 1-85345-373-0

Ecclesiastes
Hard questions and spiritual answers
ISBN-13: 978-1-85345-371-7
ISBN-10: 1-85345-371-4

1 Corinthians
Growing a Spirit-filled church
ISBN-13: 978-1-85345-374-8
ISBN-10: 1-85345-374-9

Moses
Face to face with God
ISBN-13: 978-1-85345-336-6
ISBN-10: 1-85345-336-6

2 Timothy and Titus
Vital Christianity
ISBN-13: 978-1-85345-338-0
ISBN-10: 1-85345-338-2

Rivers of Justice
*Responding to God's call to
righteousness today*
ISBN-13: 978-1-85345-339-7
ISBN-10: 1-85345-339-0

Nehemiah
Principles for life
ISBN-13: 978-1-85345-335-9
ISBN-10: 1-85345-335-8

Hebrews
Jesus – simply the best
ISBN-13: 978-1-85345-337-3
ISBN-10: 1-85345-337-4

Parables
Communicating God on earth
ISBN-13: 978-1-85345-340-3
ISBN-10: 1-85345-340-4

Hosea
The love that never fails
ISBN-13: 978-1-85345-290-1
ISBN-10: 1-85345-290-4

James
Faith in action
ISBN-13: 978-1-85345-293-2
ISBN-10: 1-85345-293-9

God's Rescue Plan
*Finding God's fingerprints on human
history*
ISBN-13: 978-1-85345-294-9
ISBN-10: 1-85345-294-7

1 Timothy
Healthy churches – effective Christians
ISBN-13: 978-1-85345-291-8
ISBN-10: 1-85345-291-2

£3.99 each (plus p&p)
Price correct at time of printing

CWR Website and Store

Visit our website store at **www.cwr.org.uk** and you can buy our products online with the safety and security of WorldPay. Offering a complete listing of all our products, our online store gives you:

• Full *Cover to Cover* product range

• Fantastic bargains, including entry to our Bargain Basement

• All our publications: seven titles of daily Bible reading notes, over 200 Christian book titles, audio-visual resources, calendars and diaries

• Your own personalised account

• Forthcoming titles

• Special offers, subscriptions and bestsellers

From the store you can also access the full range of our ministry, including Waverley training courses, news, prayer and forums. Why not visit it today?